the Living Ocean

The Ocean Biome

Kathryn Smithyman & Bobbie Kalman

Crabtree Publishing Company

www.crabtreebooks.com

the Living Ocean

Created by Bobbie Kalman

Dedicated by Kathryn Smithyman
Amanda, you are a treasure.

Editor-in-Chief
Bobbie Kalman

Writing team
Kathryn Smithyman
Bobbie Kalman

Editorial director
Niki Walker

Editors
Amanda Bishop
Molly Aloian

Copy editor
Rebecca Sjonger

Art director
Robert MacGregor

Design
Margaret Amy Reiach

Production coordinator
Heather Fitzpatrick

Photo research
Laura Hysert

Consultant
Patricia Loesche, Ph.D., Animal Behavior Program,
Department of Psychology, University of Washington

Photographs
NASA: pages 4, 10 (top)
OAR/National Undersea Research Program (NURP); College of William & Mary:
    page 21 (bottom); Univ. of Hawaii: page 30 (bottom)
Jeffrey Rotman Photography: © Jeff Rotman: pages 11 (top), 20 (top), 24
Seapics com: © Masa Ushioda: page 13 (top); © James D. Watt: page 17;
    © Peter Parks/iq3-d: page 18; © Doc White: page 20 (bottom);
    © Kevin Palmer: page 26 (top)
Tom Stack & Associates: Mike Severns: page 7 (top);
    David B. Fleetham: page 9 (bottom); Mark Allen Stack: page 27
Visuals Unlimited: © Martin Miller: page 12; © Richard Hermann: page 16;
    © Ken Lucas: page 19 (top); © HBOI: page 19 (bottom); © F. Gaill, WHOI:
    page 21 (top); © Joe McDonald: page 25
Other images by Digital Stock, Digital Vision, and Corbis Images

Illustrations
Barbara Bedell: pages 5, 8-9 (lower humpback whale), 11 (magnifying glasses), 12,
15 (right), 16, 22-23 (all except background, octopus, dead shark, plankton,
crab, and lobster), 29 (right)
Katherine Kantor: page 23 (dead shark), 27
Margaret Amy Reiach: pages 8-9 (background, octopus), 11 (plankton), 15 (left),
22-23 (background, crab, lobster, plankton, and octopus), 28
Bonna Rouse: pages 8-9 (all except background, humpback whales, octopus,
and dolphin), 29 (left), 31
Tiffany Wybouw: pages: 8-9 (upper humpback whale, and dolphin)

Crabtree Publishing Company

www.crabtreebooks.com   1-800-387-7650

PMB 16A
350 Fifth Avenue
Suite 3308
New York, NY
10118

612 Welland Avenue
St. Catharines
Ontario
Canada
L2M 5V6

73 Lime Walk
Headington
Oxford
OX3 7AD
United Kingdom

Cataloging-in-Publication Data
Smithyman, Kathryn
  The ocean biome / Kathryn Smithyman & Bobbie Kalman.
    p. cm. — (The living ocean series)
This books examines the four zones of the marine biome, their plants
and animals, coral reefs and estuaries, the importance of the oceans
to the Earth, and how they are in danger.
    ISBN 0-7787-1296-6 (RLB) — ISBN 0-7787-1318-0 (pbk.)
  1. Marine biology—Juvenile literature. [1. Marine biology.
2. Ocean.] I. Kalman, Bobbie. II. Title. III. Series.
  QH91.16.S65 2003
  577.7—dc21
                                                    2003004
                                                    LC

#

Biomes are large areas of the Earth where specific types of plants grow. The plants that grow in each biome are determined by the biome's **climate** and type of soil. Sunlight, **precipitation**, wind, and temperature are all part of a biome's climate. The animals that are found in each biome are well suited to that biome's climate. They depend on the plants that live there.

The oceans

The **aquatic**, or water-based, biome is the largest biome, covering three-quarters of the planet. It is the only biome that is not on land. It includes both **fresh water**, such as lakes and rivers, and **salt water**, such as oceans. Oceans make up the largest part of the aquatic biome.

Many ecosystems

Oceans contain many **ecosystems**. An ecosystem is made up of the plants, animals, and nonliving natural things such as sand, rocks, and soil in a certain area. There is a much wider variety of plants and animals living in oceans than in most other biomes because oceans have many ecosystems. A coral reef is one type of ocean ecosystem.

Many habitats

Within an ecosystem, plants and animals live in specific **habitats**, or natural homes. In a coral reef, for example, some fish live in the water above the coral; some hide in crevices; and others live on the ocean floor. Each location is a different habitat.

The world ocean

The world has five oceans—the Pacific, Atlantic, Indian, Southern, and Arctic Oceans—as well as many **seas**. Seas are small areas of oceans that are partly or completely surrounded by land. The oceans and seas are **interconnected**, or joined together.

Biomes of the world

- Forest biome
- Grassland biome
- Shrub and scrubland biome
- Desert biome
- Mountain biome
- Tundra biome
- Aquatic biome

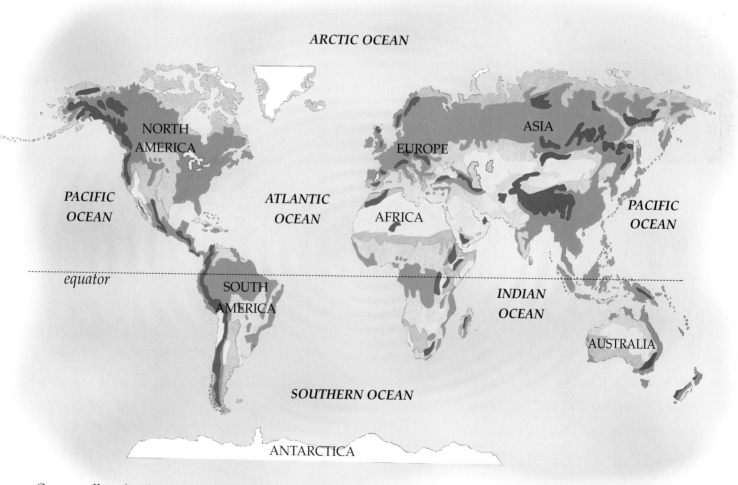

Oceans affect the climates of all land biomes. They take in heat from the sun and help create precipitation and wind. Read more about how oceans affect climate on pages 24-27.

To survive, all animals need food and oxygen. They also have to escape from **predators**. Predators are animals that hunt and eat other animals. All creatures have bodies and senses that are **adapted**, or well suited, to surviving in their biomes. **Marine** animals survive in the ocean because they are adapted to life in water. They are also adapted to their own specific habitats.

Marine animals get the oxygen they need in different ways. Water is made up of hydrogen and oxygen. Animals such as fish, corals, worms, and crustaceans use the oxygen in water. Some have thin skins that **absorb**, or take in, oxygen. Others have body parts called **gills**, which draw oxygen out of the water. Marine mammals, birds, and reptiles have lungs. They must breathe air to get oxygen.

Moving through water

Most animals must move to find food and escape from predators. Water is **denser**, or thicker and heavier, than air. It is much more difficult to move through water than it is to move through air.

The bodies of marine animals are adapted to moving in water. Many animals, such as fish, whales, rays, seals, and dolphins, use their fins and tails to **propel**, or push, themselves forward. Their sleekly shaped bodies glide easily through water.

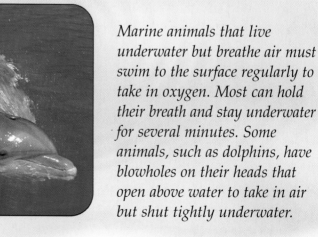

Marine animals that live underwater but breathe air must swim to the surface regularly to take in oxygen. Most can hold their breath and stay underwater for several minutes. Some animals, such as dolphins, have blowholes on their heads that open above water to take in air but shut tightly underwater.

Not so fast

Not all marine animals move by swimming. Nonswimmers need other ways to escape from predators. Some, such as crabs and lobsters, have hard shells to protect them. Others, such as octopuses, squids, and clams, propel themselves away from danger by shooting out jets of water. Many marine animals rely on **venom**, or poison, to keep enemies away. Animals may also use **camouflage** to hide from predators or **prey**. Camouflage is a color or pattern on an animal's body that allows it to blend in with its habitat.

Staying put

Some marine animals do not move at all! Sponges, corals, barnacles, and tube worms spend their lives attached to one spot. These animals do not have to search for food. It drifts past them, and they **filter**, or strain, it from the water.

Fooled by schools

Many fish swim in groups called **schools**. In a school, the fish move together and may appear to be a single large animal, which can frighten away predators. When a predator does attack, the fish scatter. Although one or two fish may be caught, most get away. Schooling also helps fish find food and avoid predators because every fish keeps an eye out for food or danger.

Zones in the ocean

Scientists study the ocean by dividing it into **zones**, or sections. One set of zones is based on the depth of the ocean. Some of these zones are named for the amount of sunlight they receive. Sunlight travels down through the water from the surface, but less and less light makes it down through each layer.

*The top layer, known as the **sunlit zone**, stretches from the surface down to 660 feet (200 m).*

*The **twilight zone** lies between 660 and 3,300 feet (200-1000 m) below the surface. Very little sunlight reaches the twilight zone. The water there is barely lit, and it is very cold.*

Ocean life

Each zone is home to different kinds of life. Plants survive only in the top layer, which is also home to the greatest number of animals. These pages show some of the animals that live in each zone. The sizes of the animals are not in correct proportion to one another.

*The **midnight zone** lies between 3,300 and 13,200 feet (1000-4000 m) below the surface. This zone and the **abyssal** waters below it are completely dark, and the temperature is barely above freezing. Abyssal waters lie between 13,200 and 19,800 feet (4000-6000 m) below the surface.*

*Some areas of the ocean floor are flat, some are mountainous, and others are deep **trenches**. These trenches can dip more than 19,800 feet (6000 m) below the ocean's surface.*

coastal zone

intertidal zone

The pelagic zone extends outward from the continental shelf.

How far from shore?

Scientists also divide the ocean into zones based on the water's distance from shore. The **intertidal zone** is along the shoreline, where the ocean washes up onto land. Beyond this zone, the land slopes into deeper water and forms a **continental shelf**. The water above the continental shelf is called the **coastal zone**. At the end of the coastal zone, the land drops away sharply and forms a steep wall called the **continental slope**, which marks the beginning of the **pelagic zone**, or open ocean.

The sunlit zone

The sunlit zone includes every part of the ocean's surface, from the intertidal zone to the pelagic zone. Unlike deeper zones, which are always cold, the water in the sunlit zone varies in temperature. Its temperature depends on where the water is in relation to the equator, as shown on the map below. Different **species**, or types, of plants and animals live in waters of different temperatures.

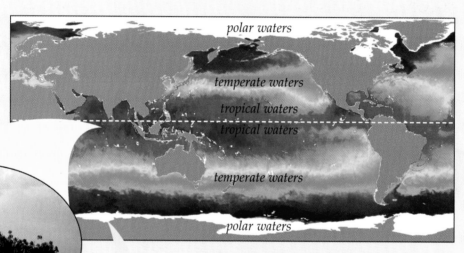

polar waters

temperate waters

tropical waters

tropical waters

temperate waters

polar waters

equator

tropical ocean

polar ocean

Hot, warm, and cold

The colored parts of the map above show the world's oceans. The colors indicate the different water temperatures of the sunlit zone. The red areas are the warmest. They are found in **tropical** areas near the equator. The white areas are the coldest. They are **polar** waters, which stay cold year-round. In the **temperate** areas between polar and tropical areas, the sunlit zone's temperature changes from season to season. It is warm in summer and cool in winter.

Green on top

Almost all ocean plants are **algae**. They live only in the sunlit zone because they need sunlight to make food. There are many types of algae. **Phytoplankton** are microscopic plants that float near the surface of deep waters. Seaweeds and kelp are other types of algae. They grow in coastal waters. Algae attract many types of plant-eating animals to the sunlit zone. Tiny animals called **zooplankton** feed on phytoplankton. Larger plant-eaters feed on kelp and seaweeds.

A type of large algae called kelp forms huge forests in some warm coastal waters.

phytoplankton

zooplankton

Loads of life

The huge numbers of **plankton**, or phytoplankton and zooplankton, in the sunlit zone attract many animals. Some eat the plankton, whereas others eat the animals that feed on plankton. Rays, sharks, squids, whales, sea turtles, sea jellies, and crustaceans all look for food in the sunlit zone.

Making waves

As wind blows across the ocean's surface, it pushes the water and creates waves. The size of a wave depends on how hard the wind is blowing. Waves do not have much of an effect on life in the pelagic zone, but they greatly affect life in the coastal and intertidal zones. Waves stir up tiny bits of food from the ocean bottom and move it throughout these zones. Every drop of water in these areas contains tiny bits of food, which attract fish and other animals.

The intertidal zone lies at the edges of continents and islands, where the ocean washes up onto land. The land, called a shore, can be a gradual slope or a steep cliff. It may be sandy, rocky, or muddy. Every day, the shore is affected by **tides**, or the rise and fall of the ocean. Tides are caused by the pull of the moon's gravity on Earth's oceans. The only coasts that do not have an intertidal zone are found in polar areas, where the shores are often covered in thick ice.

high tide at Sunset Bay, Oregon

low tide at Sunset Bay, Oregon

(left) Tides are barely noticeable away from shore, but where the ocean meets land, there can be a big difference between low tide and high tide.

Rise and fall

Conditions change constantly in the intertidal zone. At high tide, the shore is covered by water. During low tide, it is exposed to wind, waves, and sunlight. Thousands of species of plants, birds, mammals, fish, reptiles, crustaceans, and insects live in this zone. They must adjust to the changes quickly in order to survive.

Intertidal habitats

There are many types of intertidal habitats. **Tidal pools**, shown below, are dips in the shore or crevices in rocks that become filled with water from waves or high tides. Many animals, including fish, prawns, shrimps, anemones, clams, crabs, mussels, starfish, and worms, live in tidal pools. They attract many predators, including birds and raccoons. **Tidal flats** are muddy habitats covered in seagrasses. They form where streams and rivers flow into oceans. These flats are home to many types of plants, crustaceans, and birds.

Mangrove trees are adapted to living at the edge of the ocean. They have a network of roots that holds them steady in the soft sand or mud.

While the water is out during low tide, these children are investigating the living things in a tidal pool.

Each continent is surrounded by hundreds of miles of coastal zone. In various parts of the world, coastal waters have varying temperatures. Different coastal waters are home to different species of plants and animals. For example, the species of sea lions that live in the coastal waters of North America are not the same species as the sea lions that live in Australia's coastal waters.

Coastal populations

Coastal areas in some parts of the world are home to many species, whereas fewer species live in other coastal areas. **Biodiversity** is the number of different species found in an area. Tropical waters have greater biodiversity than polar waters do. Although cold waters have fewer species, they still have a lot of life. The top layer of polar waters is rich in **nutrients**, such as iron, which phytoplankton need to grow. Huge amounts of phytoplankton grow every summer in polar waters and attract swarms of zooplankton to feed. With so much plankton available to eat, the populations of other animals grow. Animals from other areas also visit polar waters to feed.

Some marine species live only in one part of the world. The Australian sea lion, above, lives only in the Pacific Ocean along the west coast of Australia.

Warm winters

Most marine animals stay in one area all their lives, but several species in the coastal zone **migrate**, or make long trips from one place to another. Some migrate every year, and others do it only once in their lifetimes. Animals migrate in order to find food or raise their young. For example, humpback whales live in the coastal waters of the Arctic Ocean in summer, where they feed on a type of zooplankton called **krill**. During the Arctic winter, however, the whales migrate to tropical coastal waters to have babies and raise their young, as shown below. As soon as spring arrives, the whales return to their Arctic home to feed.

Coral reefs

Coral reefs are ecosystems that are found only in the clear coastal waters of tropical areas. The rocky parts of a reef are formed by millions of tiny animals called **polyps**. A single coral is actually a **colony**, or group, of polyps. Each polyp has a hard **exoskeleton**, which is attached to the exoskeletons of the polyps around it. When polyps die, their exoskeletons remain.

Living on the reef

Coral reefs are full of life. They are home to more than one-quarter of all the ocean's plants and animals—including at least 4,000 species of fish. Most reef animals cannot live anywhere else in the ocean. They rely on the reef and one another for shelter and food.

Above the deep

The pelagic zone begins where a continental shelf drops away and forms a continental slope. The waters at the top of the pelagic zone are brightly lit like those of the coastal and intertidal zones. Where the pelagic zone meets the coastal zone, the waters are full of life. Plankton are plentiful there, and schools of small fish gather to feed on them. The schools attract larger fish, such as the shark shown below, as well as birds such as albatrosses, auks, and gannets, which hunt at the surface.

Further from the continental slope, there are large areas of open ocean with little plankton or none at all. Fewer animals live in these waters than in areas where plankton are plentiful.

The gannet, shown right, hunts in the Atlantic Ocean. It dives into the water to catch fish and squids.

Hiding in the light

In the sunlit waters at the top of the pelagic zone, there are no places for animals to hide. Many survive only because they are difficult to spot. Most fish have glittery scales that reflect light, making them look like flashes of sunlight in the water. Predators, including sharks and dolphins, have **countershading**, or dark backs and light bellies. When seen from above, their backs blend in with the dark water below. From below, their bellies blend in with the bright surface above.

Breathing room

All whales spend some time in the upper waters of the pelagic zone. Many species, including humpback whales, right whales, porpoises, and narwhals, live in this zone all the time. They feed on huge amounts of krill near the surface. Dolphins, orcas, and sperm whales spend time hunting at deeper levels but swim through the sunlit waters to breathe at the surface.

Far from any hiding places, these dolphins travel in large groups for protection. Predators find it harder to see and hunt an animal that is part of a group.

The waters of the twilight zone are lit dimly compared to the bright waters of the sunlit zone. The temperature is also colder, and the water is denser. Most animals are able only to swim weakly or float through these cold, dense waters. Far fewer animals live in the twilight zone than in the sunlit zone. They include some species of fish, shrimp, sea jellies, and octopuses. A few large animals, such as sperm whales, dive down to this zone to hunt.

Plants do not grow in the twilight zone. Most animals feed on leftover bits of plant and animal matter that drifts down from the sunlit zone. Twilight zone animals may go long periods without eating, since they rely on food falling from the zone above. Squids, hatchet fish, and lantern fish live in the twilight zone only during the day. They swim up to the sunlit zone to feed at night, when the waters are dark and cool.

Under pressure

The ocean presses against the bodies of underwater animals from all sides, creating **water pressure**. Water pressure increases with depth. **Gelatinous**, or jelly-like, animals such as sea jellies live in all ocean zones, including the twilight zone. The bodies of these animals are made up mostly of water, which has the same pressure as the water outside their bodies. Their bodies move through the ocean like an air-filled balloon moves through air. Sea jellies move easily through deep waters despite the pressure.

A sea jelly's body is more than 95 percent water.

Nowhere to hide

There is nowhere to hide in the twilight zone—it is a vast space without any shelter. Most animals avoid predators by being difficult to see. Many have **transparent**, or see-through, bodies. Others are dark red or black. They blend in with the dark water.

Not much to see

Many twilight zone animals that swim have bodies that are very flat and thin. This body shape makes it easier for them to slip through the dense water. Thin bodies are also more difficult to see—especially from below. Having thin bodies helps these fish go unnoticed by predators that live at the bottom of the twilight zone and swim upward to feed.

A light in the darkness

Several twilight zone animals are **bioluminescent**, or able to give off light. Their bodies contain **bacteria** that produce light. Twilight zone animals use bioluminescence in different ways. Some use it to see in the dark. Others use it to attract mates or prey. Luring prey rather than chasing it helps animals save energy.

Flashlight fish have body parts that light up. These fish live in the Indian and Pacific Oceans. They swim up to the sunlit zone at night to feed on animals that are attracted to their light organs.

Hatchet fish have large eyes to help them see prey in the dimly lit waters. These fish have light organs on their undersides, which may help protect them from enemies. Predators swimming below them may mistake the lights for flashes of sunlight from the surface.

The darkest depths

Most of the water in the ocean is far below the surface in the midnight zone. There is absolutely no light in these waters, and the temperatures are near freezing. Conditions are always the same—this zone is too deep to be affected by sunlight, storms at the surface, or changing seasons. There are no plants, so despite its vast size, this zone is home to fewer animals than are the zones above it. The deep water is very dense, and the water pressure is very strong. There is so much pressure that most large animals would be crushed if they ventured down into this zone. A few species of octopuses, sea jellies, and eels do survive in these depths because they are smaller and thinner than the species that live in the waters above them.

Bodies in the deep

Deep ocean fish may look fearsome, but most are fewer than two inches (5 cm) long. They survive the cold and the water pressure by remaining still. The fish do not swim to chase prey but, instead, wait for food to swim by or sink from above. Many have big mouths to catch food and stomachs that expand to hold a lot of food when it is available. Deep ocean fish such as angler fish have upturned mouths because all their food falls from above. Many animals, such as the amphipod below, do not have eyes! Eyesight is useless in the black water.

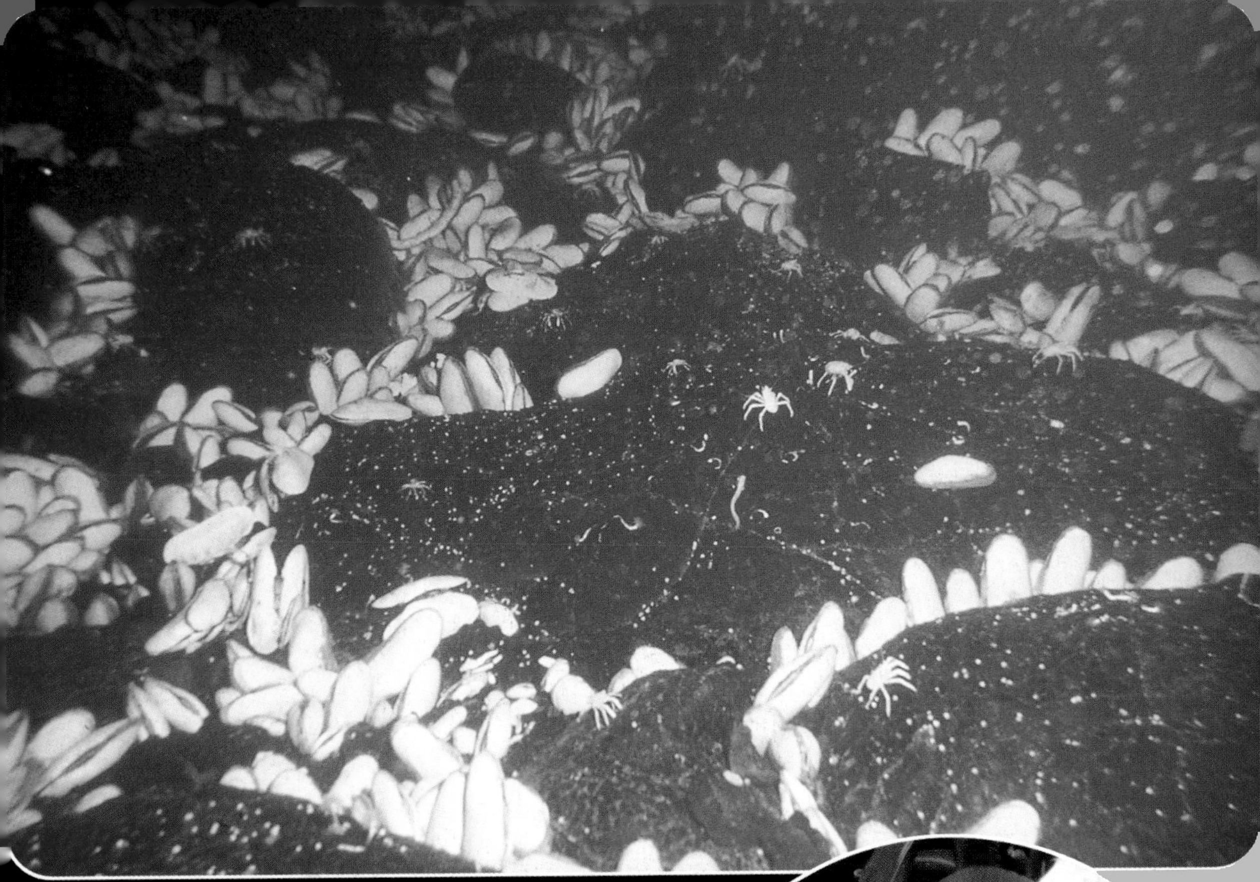

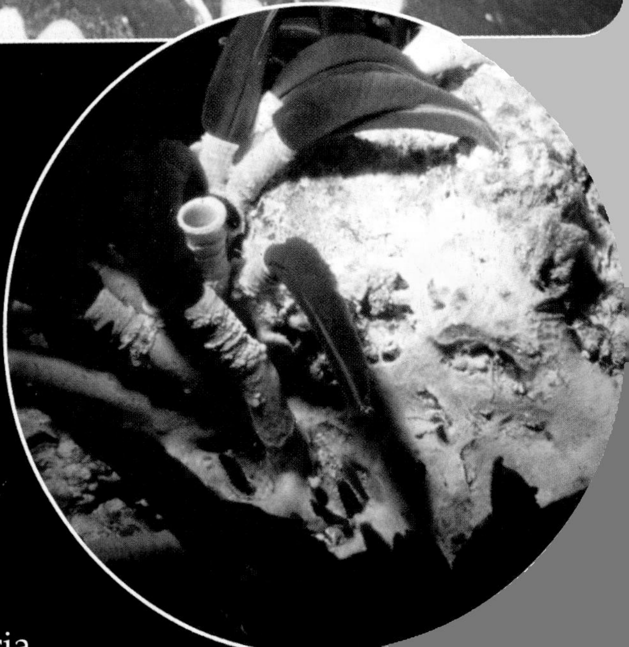

Vent communities

Few creatures live in abyssal waters. Most of those that survive at these depths live around **hydrothermal vents**, or openings that let out heat and gases from inside the Earth. Bacteria found in abyssal waters can make food from chemicals in the gases. Other living things, such as the crabs and clams shown above, and the tube worms, shown right, feed on the bacteria.

Living things need energy to grow, move, reproduce, and to defend themselves. Plants are the only living things that can turn the sun's energy into food. In the ocean, phytoplankton and other algae use water, nutrients, and sunlight to make food.

Energy from above

All ocean animals rely on the food energy that algae makes. **Herbivores**, or animals that eat plants, get energy directly from the algae. Most feed on tiny bits of phytoplankton while swimming through the water. **Carnivores** eat other animals to get energy. When a carnivore eats a herbivore, energy passes to the carnivore. The movement of energy is shown by the yellow arrows in the picture. The pattern of eating and being eaten is called a **food chain**. Most animals eat more than one type of plant or animal, so many food chains are connected to one another. Connected food chains form a **food web**.

shark

barracuda

parrotfish

coral

22

Cleaning up

The ocean floor is rich in nutrients. Pieces of food left over from animals feeding above drift down, as do animal **wastes**, which contain nutrients. The bodies of dead animals also sink to the bottom. **Scavengers**, such as lobsters and crabs, eat the bodies of dead animals they find.

Many bacteria are **decomposers** that feed on the leftover bits of plants and animals. With their wastes, decomposers release nutrients that would otherwise be trapped in dead plants and animals. When nutrients move from the ocean floor to the surface, algae uses them to make food. This cycle keeps the food chain going.

plankton

butterfly fish

octopus

squid

puffer fish

crab

dead shark

lobster

Oceans in motion

Currents are like giant rivers of water that flow through oceans. Some currents flow at the surface, whereas others move in the deep waters. Currents are caused by winds, heat from the sun, and the rotation of Earth. Winds cause currents at the ocean's surface, which flow mainly in an east-to-west direction. The Earth's rotation causes currents that **circulate**, or flow around the Earth, in the deep ocean.

The sun's heat causes currents that flow away from the equator to the poles and back again. A lot of heat enters tropical oceans, causing the waters to **expand**, or spread. The warm waters form currents that spread out from the equator toward the poles. These currents push cold polar waters out of the way and force them back toward the equator. They **moderate**, or even out, the temperature of the oceans.

Up from the bottom

Some ocean currents move up and down between different depths. These movements are created by changes in water density. Temperature and **salinity**, or the amount of salt in water, changes the density of water. Polar waters, which are cold and salty, are denser than tropical waters, which are warm and less salty. When cold polar waters flow toward the equator, they meet warmer waters. The polar waters sink all the way to the ocean floor because they are so dense.

As the cold water sinks, it pushes the water at the bottom out of the way. When water from the bottom is pushed upwards, it carries nutrients from the ocean floor up with it. This upward movement of nutrient-rich water is called **upwelling**. Upwelling plays an important role in feeding ocean animals. Huge amounts of plankton grow where the nutrient-rich waters reach the surface. Many animals, including the humpback whales shown below, feed in these waters.

All marine plants and animals depend on currents for their survival. Currents move nutrients throughout the oceans. When nutrients are carried to the surface, algae use them to make food energy.

Climate control

Oceans are so enormous that they affect conditions in all other biomes. No living things, not even desert creatures, could survive without them! Oceans absorb a great deal of heat from the sun. Currents moderate ocean temperatures and also affect the heating of the whole planet. Without oceans and their currents, tropical land areas, shown above, would be too hot, and polar regions, shown left, would be too cold for plants and animals to survive.

Keep it moving

Oceans help keep Earth's **water cycle**, shown below, working. As the sun heats ocean water, some of it **evaporates**, or changes from a liquid to a gas called **vapor**. When vapor rises, it cools and forms water droplets that join together and become clouds. When clouds get too dense, the water droplets fall as rain. Most rain falls into oceans, but rain that falls on land helps the plants and animals living there survive. By creating precipitation, oceans influence the climate of all other biomes.

Oceans play a key part in maintaining Earth's climate. When heat escapes from the oceans, it rises as warm air and pushes cooler air out of the way. This movement creates winds. Winds move rain and heat to different parts of the planet.

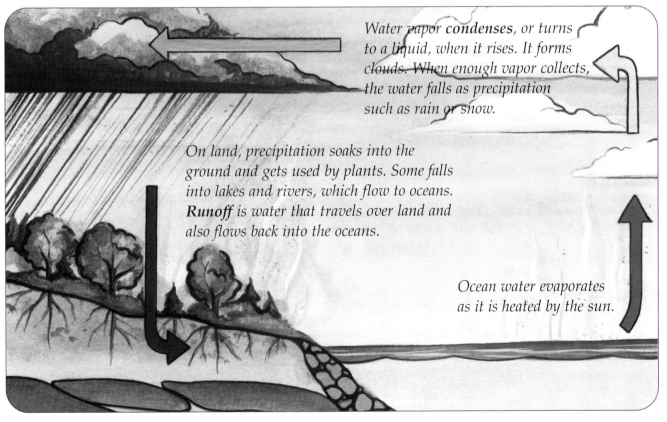

*Water vapor **condenses**, or turns to a liquid, when it rises. It forms clouds. When enough vapor collects, the water falls as precipitation such as rain or snow.*

*On land, precipitation soaks into the ground and gets used by plants. Some falls into lakes and rivers, which flow to oceans. **Runoff** is water that travels over land and also flows back into the oceans.*

Ocean water evaporates as it is heated by the sun.

Oceans in danger

Marine plants and animals are well adapted to their habitats when the oceans are in their natural states. People's actions change the natural conditions of oceans, however. The changes damage habitats and threaten the survival of the plants and animals living in them. People dump tons of trash, sewage, and chemicals into the oceans. These things do not belong there and upset the natural balance of ocean habitats, causing plants and animals to become ill or to develop diseases. Many animals choke when they eat trash that they mistake for prey. Others get tangled in garbage and drown.

People problems

*People around the world fish for cod, tuna, sharks, lobsters, whales, and many other marine animals. **Overfishing**, or taking too many of one species from an area, upsets the balance of ocean food webs. It may even cause a species to become **extinct**.*

Oil spills are disasters for ocean life. The sticky oil coats plants and animals, and many animals drown. Some become sick from eating the oil. Others starve because the oil poisons the plants on which they rely for food.

Pollution causes diseases in many ocean animals. People who eat diseased animals may also get sick.

Careless snorkelers and divers damage, or even kill, coral by touching, kicking, or standing on it. Never touch coral—even gently!

Overheating

The biggest threat to oceans is **global warming**, or the rising of the temperature of Earth. It is caused by too many **greenhouse gases**, especially carbon dioxide, being released into the air. Carbon dioxide is produced by burning fossil fuels such as coal, oil, and gasoline. People burn these fuels to heat their homes and to run cars, trucks, trains, and factories.

*There may be millions of plant and animal species in the ocean—far more than scientists have studied. Many unknown species may be **endangered** or already extinct.*

Too close to the edge!

Coastal and intertidal habitats are damaged or destroyed when people build housing and resorts on them. These areas are important feeding and breeding grounds for many ocean animals such as sea turtles, whales, and countless types of birds.

Sea turtles rely on the position of the moon to tell the right time and place to lay eggs. Bright lights around beaches confuse sea turtles, and they do not lay eggs.

Care for coral

About half the fish in the oceans rely on coral reefs for food and shelter, but many reefs are now in danger of dying out. Around the world, more and more reefs are **bleaching**. Coral bleaches when it is under stress. Scientists believe the greatest stress is the unnatural warming of oceans. Pollution may also cause some bleaching. Corals sometimes recover after bleaching if the source of their stress disappears. When stress lasts more than a few months, however, bleached reefs die.

Exploring the ocean can be challenging for **oceanographers**, or scientists who study oceans. Studying deep water habitats is especially difficult because darkness, cold temperatures, and intense water pressure make it impossible for divers to swim down to these areas. Divers must travel inside expensive deep-diving vehicles. Many scientists rely on a variety of robotic equipment to photograph the ocean floor, take measurements, and record information.

Scuba divers can explore the ocean floor only in coastal areas.

Detecting depth

Oceanographers measure ocean depth using **sonar**. Scientists know that the speed of sound in water is about 4,921 feet (1500 m) per second. Sonar equipment directs a sound into the water and measures the time it takes for the sound to travel to the ocean bottom and then bounce back.

*Scientists use **submersibles**, or deep-water vehicles, to explore very deep water. This submersible holds one person and can travel to a depth of 984 feet (300 m). Some submersibles can travel even deeper.*

Getting wise

More and more people recognize the importance of oceans as homes to many unique and necessary living things. In some areas, scientists, governments, and other people have joined together to establish protected areas in the water. One is the Great Barrier Reef Marine Park, which stretches along the northeast coast of Australia.

Helping out

There are things you can do every day that will benefit oceans. Anything you can do to reduce pollution and global warming helps them. Find out about groups in your area or around the world that are working to preserve oceans and marine plants and animals. Learn about endangered ocean habitats that need protection and decide how you can get involved!

Check it out

Check out these websites to learn more about the importance of the aquatic biome to all living things—including you!

- http://www.mos.org/oceans
- http://oceanlink.island.net
- http://www.worldbiomes.com
- http://www.oceanconservancy.org

Glossary

Note: Boldfaced words that are defined in the book may not appear in the glossary.

algae Green plants without stems and leaves that grow in water

bacteria Microscopic single-celled living things

bleaching The process in which coral polyps release the algae on which they rely to make food

climate The long-term weather conditions in an area, including temperature, rainfall, and wind

current An area of an ocean that moves continuously in a certain direction

endangered Describing an animal or plant species that is in danger of dying out

exoskeleton The hard shell-like covering that protects the outside of an invertebrate's body

extinct Describing a plant or animal species that no longer exists on Earth

gills The body part that an aquatic animal uses to remove oxygen from the water

greenhouse gases Gases such as carbon dioxide that trap heat within the Earth's atmosphere

marine Describing animals that live in the ocean; describing areas of the ocean

nutrient A natural substance that helps plants and animals grow

polar Describing an area around the North or South Pole that has a cold climate

polyp A tiny marine animal with a soft round body and tentacles around its mouth

precipitation Water, such as rain, snow, or hail, that falls from the sky to the Earth's surface

prey An animal that is hunted and eaten by other animals

sonar An instrument that sends out radio waves to discover and locate objects under the water

temperate Describing areas with mild climates between the tropical and polar regions

trench A steep-sided valley on the ocean floor

tropical Describing areas with hot climates found near near the equator

waste Undigested material that is eliminated from the body

Index

1 2 3 4 5 6 7 8 9 0 Printed in the U.S.A. 2 1 0 9 8 7 6 5 4 3